# CREATIVE WRITING WORKSHOP

# CREATIVE WRITING WORKSHOP

*Ignite Your Imagination*

BILL VINCENT

QuantumQuill Press

# CONTENTS

# CHAPTER 1

# Introduction

What do you think a writer should do to be successful? The answer is very simple. This is it. How, Where, What and When. You don't believe me, do you? How are you going to carry out the experiment I want you to do? Where are you going to do this experiment? What is it and when are you going to do that experiment? Whether you are sitting all alone by yourself, with your best friend or in a classroom with your teacher, these questions trace the outlines of the literary journey, a journey as vast and wondrous as the universe, a journey as familiar and as difficult as the pattern of your life. Now do you believe me?

Bonjour to everyone! This is your Creative Writing Workshop. If you are looking for something fun and exciting, you have come to the right place. Here is where you will learn the basic skills to get you started in your life as a writer. Okay, now I am going to tell you a secret. Every one of us, myself included, is an aspiring writer. When you were young, you would have written letters to your family or friends, right? Or when you went on holidays, you would have written in your travel diary. What about or e-mail accounts? Telephone SMS messages? These are all boxes for writers and they help provoke the writer in each of us.

*1.1. Overview*

You must be ready to improve your creative side while, at the same time, keeping your strict evaluation inclinations at bay. This is not an academic writing programme, but a creative one. One of the biggest excuses in life not to write is lack of time. Setting aside time to regularly tap into the creative side of your brain is the only way you are going to be able to effectively push through your writer's block and actually write. It's also one of the only things you can do to force your brain into the writing zone. Once you are tapping away at the keys of your laptop, the words will flow. This course is specifically designed to force you into the writing zone.

During the intensive 4-day programme, you will learn to write each morning, then get feedback afterwards. This is a practical, writing-intensive course, designed to get your creative ideas onto the written page. In the afternoon, listen to writers who have succeeded in getting their work published as they take you through their writing experience, give you tips and answer your burning questions. Last year one participant went home and won a writing competition! Set your imagination free while writing about a topic that concerns us all - water. Last year's participants were between the ages of 20 and 68, making for interesting debates and presentations. You also need to be available to attend the evening programme every day.

# CHAPTER 2

# Importance of Creative Writing

At this conference, I hope, the paper that I am presenting today on the importance of creative writing will awaken the authorities of the schools and colleges. I request them to give every encouragement to creative writing, which is the basis for the development of a country. This conference on creative writing will help to awaken their dormant consciousness. Those who are attending this conference should go to the Department of Education and prevail upon the professors to give every encouragement to the subject. I appeal and request the authorities of the Board of the University to give 25 marks for poetry. This is to have some standard for creative writing. Unless the conjurations of the developers are not in harmony with the artists, literature, the result in human life will become lower and worse. I appeal to the Press to help us raise the subjects to a high pedestal because it has its influence on the nations. I also appeal to the poets and writers who are now at the mercy of others to improve themselves, spend some time to improve their art so that the literature will be at a high standard. I hope that the present conference will be a grand success.

Creative writing is becoming extinct in schools and colleges of our cities. No one seems to show any interest in it. The teachers, as well as the taught, seem to be more taken up with material things. The present-day education does not encourage a child to write verses or imaginative pieces. The bright students are encouraged to write their term papers in prose in such a manner that the teacher may award them good marks. All the Head Masters of schools and colleges and the Vice Chancellors of universities think that Latin and Science subjects are more beneficial than the study of poetry and literature.

## 2.1. Benefits

Participants learn about the six rights of writing—the habits of the mind that can lead writers in any direction they want—and did free writing exercises that asked them to imagine their senses in a different part of the body. Veterans also bring a lot to the table, Dietz said, referring to clinical psychiatric work she's done for 22 years. "One defining factor of many recipients of care in the mental health service is conflict with the body, conflict with one's own mind, with one's life's experiences," she said. "This creative writing opportunity provides veterans with the chance to process substantial life experiences." Participants complete their drafts by the end of the session and have the unique opportunity to finish a piece based on feedback from a McDaniel College president. That is important, Dietz said, because most veterans "will assume the negative space."

Creative writing has the potential to help veterans in good ways, a VA Puget Sound Health Care System doctor said. "It reaches the part of the brain that maybe hasn't quite entered into the recovery mode yet and provides that safe and shared experience in writing," Dr. Elizabeth Dietz said. "You get the connections and the communities and you have less isolation and disconnection." At the end of February, Dr. Dietz and Dr. Roger Casey, president of McDaniel College in Maryland, partnered with the MediXL Project to pilot a creative writing workshop with a group of veterans at the Ft. Meade, Maryland, VA outpatient clinic. Participants practiced writing exercises, shared their stories and got the chance to have their work critiqued by Casey.

## 2.2. Impact on Imagination

For those at both amateur and professional level, writing has always allowed me to explore, pass examinations, and discover the processes of learning. Writing is a symbolic preoccupation. This means that the writing is a way to relate to something else. However, a unique meaning involves substitution. We use symbols to represent. Writing to transcribe replaces things and feelings that cannot be expressed in other ways. This is why programs such as expressive writing workshops have been proven to enrich people's thoughts with creative and transformative positive experiences, and with one another.

Imagination provides a vital evolutionary advantage. The capacity to think abstractly is linked to progress in essential thinking skills, and imagination provides opportunities for social understanding. Imagination celebrates independence, tolerates successful problem solving, and presents ideas of power and control over what is remembered from long-term memory. Derived from real-life experiences and interests, imagination ignites retaliatory comprehension. A kind of vision and determination cause creativity. In due course, ideas go from hypothesis to reality.

# CHAPTER 3

# Elements of Creative Writing

3. Imagination - a complete overview of the work is revealed in the author's head. However, it should be noted that it is not enough to have an idea, since there is always fear of creative writing anyway, and when they write about the problems discussed below, authors begin to lose energy and determination over time. In such moments, you should return to your initial idea. The beauty of the idea can always be useful. Do not forget to give your imagination time to think about all the intricacies, smallest details and inconsistencies.

2. Idea - involves initial planning and analysis. In his mind, the author is trying to construct the whole of the planned work, or at least its skeleton. When this process is lengthy and difficult, it is called creativity. In order to accelerate the search for a path to the mind and thereby open an approach to the source of creative inspiration, various methods and techniques of creative imagination have been developed. However, finding an idea by quickly and easily determining the paths to the mind that lead to the source of creative inspiration and methods of realization of the creative search leads to the formation of creative thinking. In other words, for an idea, the invention or discovery of an object, idea or techniques, useful physical laws for realization are

revealed. When important ideas are developed, these can generate new creative projects.

1. Impulse - the lowest stage of creation, the emergence of an idea. This is often an event or revelation that excites and inspires the author. Here, a typical phrase springs to mind: "And what if...". What follows is thought or reflection. Most authors write about topics that have affected them personally.

### 3.1. Character Development

In writing we don't get the visual input so quickly and generally that happens via the senses. If a character is hiding in a garden, you have a visual image. What does it sound like? The smell of the mint—what does it bring to mind? The taste of the leaves, what's it like? Is the nib of our fountain pen a light point in the middle of her world of darkness? ...the way her fingers navigate along the slit of moonlight on the cottage wall. These questions from the senses are of transcendence importance in our characters' dressing. A simple moonlight holds our pen nib, but the experience that is of crying havoc with your life in a way nothing ever had, is envisaged by all of our character's feeling of disenchantment, the very essence of why she came to this place. No fuller characterization of her mission exists with just as few words.

From setting, which gives us the when as well as the where, a wealth of information spills out that will enable us to fill in the who—the characters in. How they dress, groom, and speak is influenced by the time and place. There are also the problems they could experience or the pleasures they may gain, all of these can be opportunities for conflict—or opening to Luke Skywalker wide vistas for growth that will help our characters change.

Are you ready to give life to your characters? Not just any life, but the life given to a frog when kissed by a princess! Here's how we create the most compelling characters we can by showing and not telling, and so give them a healthy and attractive glow just as if they were inhabiting the pages of their own fairy tales and legends.

### 3.2. Plot Building

There are also basic issues that need to be considered when plotting. These issues are generally used to classify the plots into: conflict, chance and problem. Such basic issues determine the beginning, middle, and end of our history. If you plan your story, remember to create an outline that contains every scene of your story. Such an attitude will be most advantageous in view of your story development. Then, when it is your outline you have created scenes, it is not difficult until the end of it give birth to a real literary masterpiece. Thank you.

Often, when we sit down to write a story we have a vague idea of where we want to go, and we just write as we go along to see how our story unfolds. The usual result is that we deviate from the initial idea and our story grows into something we did not expect. This is what is called writing by the seat of your pants. If you are lucky then something interesting develops, but while doing this sometimes we end with many weak spots in the plot. If you decide to sit down and plan your novel or short story then there are some forms where you can make invent or inspire, it can also be done with other people's novels. Plot building in fact can make you a stronger writer. Being able of planning a story still an important exercise, because in reality no one pays to do it a plot for others.

You can structure an interesting and exciting story by taking a few decisions such as using omniscient voice or the use of "I" voice to narrate your story. And also there exists different kinds of plots such as called conflict, that plots are simple and organic plots, chance and problem plagiarism.

### 3.3. Setting Creation

The writer's task is to make the reader feel that he or she is right there where things are happening at that moment. It is essential to choose wisely the scenery where the story will take place. The description of the scenery has to be accessible and inspiring all at the same time. The best way to practice will be to choose four of the following situations and to decide, apart from writing some characteristics for the event, what kind of scenery is better for each situation: A love or hate atmosphere; Under 10°C; A fast and elusive chase; Something smooth and various; A flight of birds; Raising your voice when you have a special respiratory disease; A seventh wedding anniversary. As it happens with characters, there are no impossible formulas to pass in a satisfactory way; you will have to experiment, in the same way as we suggest you to do with characters.

Workshop 3.3. Setting Creation There are two main aspects that students have to concentrate on in creating a setting: the physical environment and the social environment. The physical environment consists of the structure in which the action will take place (whether they are houses, rooms, or any other kind of space), the weather, the time of day, the place in which the scene takes place, and the date (there are settings which imply the strategic fact of taking place in some season or celebration). Creating places that sound familiar is the key to involve the reader into the plot straight away. The characters will move in a place that has to become familiar to the reader. The writer has to pay attention to the tiniest details: what color, what material, what shape and what smells everything has. There is a time and a place for any action, and that is precisely the task of the writer, to look for the time and place for each action. The weather has to be matched to the moment: if you have to talk about a romantic date, a rainy day might be really inspirational.

# CHAPTER 4

# Writing Techniques

Mind storming can be used to jump-start your writing. Storming the mind involves thinking up ideas as quickly as possible and writing them down as quickly as possible. Write for as long as you can keep coming up with new ideas. If you start to slow down, stop and read over what you have written so far and it might trigger more ideas. Keep writing till you are empty of ideas. Mind storming is useful for generating star quality ideas. A star quality idea is so unique or topical, everyone will find it interesting. Like star quality ideas, pockets of time are worth looking for to help develop your own writing project. Pockets of time are small units of time mostly overlooked by the average person. Small units of time, also called 'pockets of time', are available throughout your day. Chances are, if you are in the study room, you are a frequent reader, an active imaginer or an ideas person. You think up ideas with little prompts. Collect these little prompts in a repository. Watch and notice these small episodes and make note of them. These are your pockets of time prompting you while you are doing something else. Use them to develop your own writing project.

I can't teach creativity, but I can provide some writing techniques to stimulate your imagination. Word banks can be used whenever you are stuck for an idea. Anyone who knows a good selection of words has a basic toolkit of ideas to draw on. You can make up your own lists of words and keep adding to them whenever you encounter a new word. You can also get into the habit of mind storming every day.

*4.1. Point of View*

If you position your narrator as one of the main players in the story, avoid being intrusive and acknowledge impressions that may differ from your character's own. Little Red Riding Hood, for instance, probably has a hard time appreciating the Wolf's good qualities until she confronts the revelation of his fear of the Big Bad Woodsman. She sits stunned while the Wolf drops the woman's dress she had on as she stumbles further. By the time the woodsman arrives and marketing a bad man notice that promotes the oak door instead and the man's curiously oversized forearm, Little Red didn't have the heart to contradict. When writing your protagonist's narrative, energies should not be wasted in creating distracting commentary regarding the validity of their word, as in the case of Little Red. During presentation of concerned descriptions of their speech and demeanor, the protagonist's role and the world of their story in its entirety should ensure any deficit is effectively balanced.

Point of view: Whose story is it anyway? When you reflect on the narrative tradition you were primed with as you grew up, the answer to this query might be misrepresenting in the simplicity it conveys: the characters tell their stories, right? The Big Bad Wolf blows it, Red Riding Hood sets the facts straight, and the pigs cry for justice, all the while Mama and an eccentric group of strangers recount a confounding tale. But what of the chickens? And the mole? The ants and the caterpillar? The story you are told is really a reflection of doctrine of perspectives, impacted by and ultimately held to the viewpoints of a select few. We are omitted the other participants in the narrative, the very background from which the event tale springs. It's in this absence, more than any presence, that Little Red stands out as a cherished character. These are the overlooked elements that could provide a storytelling experience that extends beyond critique and editing. Little Red Riding Hood's story belongs to her, as do all the other players' testimonies, but hers is only one of a world of stories, and sometimes, it's the least believable, the onlooker's truth that comes out in the end.

*4.2. Dialogue*

Conversely, as your speaker is giving voice to himself, how much of the content comes from the people your speaker is addressing? How do the words of the other characters reveal their voices, preoccupations, accents, and their interaction with your speaker? If two speakers are sharing a common opening, what different inflections might they display? Listen to the accents in your skull, and record the opportunities for paradox and miscommunication and poignancy that exist. Go to museums or people's homes and observe how so many different kinds of people speak to the ones they love the most, and recall not just the words they use but their body language, gesture, hesitation, off-the-menu-reactions, speed, and the hints of emotional orientation. A longer slice of dialogue is given to Ian McEwan in his short story "On the Train".

The purpose of dialogue is to reflect natural-sounding speech and to provide the reader with a sense of the speaker without explicitly announcing the identity of the house guest. It is to suggest the character's personality, tension, humor, and interests simply by the words employed by the character, and by the style of the delivery. What does your dialog reveal about your speaker? What does it say about whom she/ he is speaking to? Is the speaker male or female, young or old, urban or rural, of a different race? What is the speaker wearing, thinking, hinting at? Does the character interject thoughts ("Uh, well..."), or does he/she seem to lack thought?

*4.3. Descriptive Language*

There are certain words people would use. That doesn't mean you are confined to one type of vocabulary for your characters – people can change, and their attitude could show it – but be consistent, and consider your audience. Connotation – or 'the extra meaning': Words often have two sets of meaning. Denotations are the dictionary meanings and connotations are the emotional meanings of words that you would often apply to certain situations or people. The connotations of a word, therefore, may change depending on the individual reader's experience. For example, the word 'home' would naturally bring out warm, domestic emotions from the reader.

Simile is a figure of speech depending on some sort of parallel between two things. So you can write about 'a face as beautiful as a rose', or 'a storm as heavy as a rucksack'. Personification is a figure of speech in which human characteristics are attributed to an abstract concept, a non-human object or animal qualities or form. This could be as simple as saying, 'the rain started to cry'. However remember, this is difficult to get right! And, if it's done wrong, it will not communicate the right thing to your reader. This is why you need to be specific. Instead of letting your reader make their own mind about the character's personality, give your characters a voice that will tell the reader what kind of person they're dealing with.

Creative writing captures the reader's imagination. In order to keep your reader engaged, it's worth remembering that if you can create a clear picture or scenario in their mind's eye of what's happening, they are more likely to keep turning the page. One way to do this is through descriptive language. The focus of this section is on identifying different writing techniques to create images or communicate character traits or emotions. Metaphor is a word or a phrase used to describe something when you are speaking of it as if it were something else or as if it possessed a quality that it does not have.

# CHAPTER 5

# Finding Inspiration

Creative writing is not necessarily the great concept or a scene from a novel. You cannot find paintings of mixed media and self-portraits, for example, making some stand-out items which express your personality. This is an astonishing way to boost you. Your friends and family will encourage you if you are dedicated to creating self-portraits together. While alone or during work with your workshop, or with other people's mixed media enterprises, there will be an innovative combination of colored pencils, paints and textiles to excite the others! A picture really is worth a thousand words to those of us habitually immersed in words and texts. Don't fret. When you start discussing these visual images, the descriptions will settle in – just focus on that. Perhaps you will dig further into your new story! With these supplies, the forward writing generates so many images and themes! Now that you are working on developing your creativeness, the choices are endless.

It does not need to be a natural phenomenon for us to be as creatively inspired as we may be by a grand sunset or at an awesome view. Though the classics are always essential, you can take things a (literal) step further by making an imaginative work of your own. New life can be breathed into your piece of work. While alone, in a group or when leading one of your classes, some unbelievable works of art can be made when trying this experiment. To create a fantastic story for you and/or your family to read and give you a sense of fantasy in the process, try a little creative writing for people of all ages. You do not know where your creativeness can take you for as long as you keep rooted in a specific moment.

### 5.1. Prompts

Prompts can be sensational – they can stimulate our senses! Today was a hot, hazy, and almost non-wind day, and I found myself lying on the soft, warm earth beside my pond. A weak yet sweet breeze waffled through the Weeping Willow, drawing zigzags through the grey ashes on the pile of tree prunings. Each visitation of breeze gave the piled ashes lifelike movement. Bamboo chimes sang a joyous song while yellow-winged swallows joyfully symphony that seemed to mock my introspective mood and speaks openly for free-form expression. This was the day that I learned to expect the unusual. The day is becoming a delightful uproar of sense as I begin to write. The feel of the overload is slow, warm, and dull. I feel its muted energy mixed with a profound and wonderful peace. The smell of decaying vegetation is mild and almost sweet, distinct, and different from the normal scent of leaves. The turkey's beasing inf limitation is flora. The sound slits the air and resounds in white and extraordinary flourishes all around the yard. The birds tweet, coo, sing, and anns. Our earth rains. I am bespoke.

Some of the major proponents of writing expressive kinds of writing are Peter Elbow, Ken Macrorie, and Donald Murray. These writers were creative teachers who valued imaginative thought and encouraged student authors to take risks as they searched for new and unique ideas. They encouraged students to start with exploratory writing, usually short, and use this writing as a means of learning about ideas – their ideas. According to these authors, in order to succeed as writers, students need to be able to see how writing can take them to places that they would never reach without experience support themselves, and experimental writing must be valued. It all begins with exploratory writing!

*5.2. Observation*

Exercise 1: Begin with a list of every descriptive word, phrase or clause you can to describe a pear. Exercise 2: Using the same list, write a poem or a paragraph about a random thought topic of your own choosing, this time making use of every image from your list of what a pear looks like. How has the structure of what you made evoked a shape similar to a pear? Conversely, can you uncover longer or broader descriptions of other objects broken into a succession of pear-shaped images? Try to think of greater descriptive elements, kinetic and emotive ones. What roles do these elements fulfill themselves that pear shapes could not?

5.2. Observation - Carefully notice and look at how things appear. The smallest detail might inspire you. When you look at something carefully, you are also giving yourself enough material to describe how it appears. Description is the key to allowing your reader to feel comfortable and confident that he or she knows what you are writing about. No writer is so important as to escape the necessity of describing what they have in mind before they can get into more highfalutin prose or narrative. Before we can engage with what a writer is saying, we have to know what the writer is describing.

# CHAPTER 6

# Overcoming Writer's Block

Another writer's block advice is to take a little piece of dust from your room and allow your imagination to conjure up an entire world from it. It might be a piece of dirt on the floor from the last tenant or cellulose. You can imagine that the cellulose has come to life or is trying to communicate with you, the witness. The cellulose might be expressing its sorrow for human kind because it can see many things that we can't, because it was once a conscious human observer too. Once in class, students saw a tiny toy soldier and suddenly the students were writing two stories. The soldier wants to go on leave and wants to take home with him. The student's voices softened as they visualized the colonel in boots cleaning his shako, asking other soldiers on leave to bring home together because lonely soldiers should go home together as one family. The dust particles seen that evening, had for a few seconds, become soldiers. In the second instance, the soldiers caught in home away from the sleep away death. The students read their stories out loud with the voice of deep feeling readers.

Overcoming writer's block is a difficult task, but can be attempted with the help of others or alone. Primarily, you must follow the rules – don't answer any emails or check your text messages or fix, correct or spell check. Your goal is to just keep writing without stop. Start writing in the evening and don't allow any distractions from the television or internet. You can also close your eyes so most of your energy is concentrated in visual imagery. Closing your eyes allows you to focus on the endless possibility of stories. It has an advantage because you are forced to enter a kind of tunnel vision. Don't stop writing until the clock says – three in the morning or the sun begins to shine through your curtains.

*6.1. Strategies*

Be open-minded. Be adventurous. Limit yourself to a word count, and try to finish your piece for the day. At the end of the week, go back and count which one you liked and disliked the most. Then, think about how the opposite piece would have gone, or try re-writing it. Get yourself into the habit of writing every day, the word count goal will help you with writer's block. Don't edit your piece as you go; just let it out. Editing comes after, if you want to. Be open to other perspectives - think about somebody else's point of view and write about it.

Write every day. Keep a journal or a notebook everywhere you go. Write about how you're feeling; write about the way things look or about how you see something or someone; write about something you found; write about something you misplaced or lost; write about something you tasted. Write about what you're afraid of; what you're anxious about; what you're excited for. Write about dreams. On top of the page, write a sentence about one thing you really want to happen. Tell yourself that it's a true sentence, and get writing.

# CHAPTER 7

# Peer Review and Feedback

The last day of the workshop will focus on genre fiction, one of our most popular sessions. Workshop is an excellent exercise in communicating one's ideas through writing, in English, in the workshop forums, and through synchronous video workshops. Thoughtful and constructive feedback will be provided to the participants. What is constructive feedback? It expresses an honest appraisal of the work, but also acknowledges the effort behind it and the strengths of the work. More often, we will need to start with a simple acknowledgment. Try to think of one item of the writer's work that is working. Participating in a creative writing work does not require any previous experience or published work. The workshop will be synchronous meetings, and the final projects will be based on participation. Active participation then is required. A lack of participation may decrease your final grade or even result in your loss of lodging and meal benefits.

Please note that, due to the pandemic, no in-person meetings will happen this term. All students must be available for live lectures at the scheduled time (unless a recording option is possible, it is not guaranteed). Encourages students to attend more than one live session if possible in case any technical difficulties result in a session being cut short. There are now many ways in which the craft of writing can be discussed, deconstructed, and learned. Peer review and feedback are cornerstones in any writing courses; members of our workshop will be trained in giving constructive feedback to their peers and will have received a good number of responses for their weekly writing except for the last day. The main feedback will have a focus on the author's improvement in future projects. This will improve not only feedback givers, but also the author from different points of view. It is always important to listen to examples of works in progress and how they can improve. We will discuss storytelling, character progressions, dialogues, narrative voice discovery and the use of inspiration in those works.

### 7.1. Importance

Importance is a subjective concept in the literature, emphasizing that the individual may feel great relevance for something considered important, and another individual can see insignificant, disregarding that being the result of making various associations. This means that the notion of importance is a result of personal, historical, cultural and social experiences. In relation to early childhood education, creative and imaginative practices can contribute to the child's interest in reading and the written word, assisting in aesthetic sensibility and personal experience with the texts, fiction, real, orality, and images, to literary education of children, and the avoided school dropout. The proposal to investigate indications arising from teachers about literary education in preschool years echoes the daily experiences and imaginative use of knowledge and objects of infantile fiction that takes place in these spaces. It discusses the relevance of these "life events" for the children's process of developing a literary sensitivity to expand the horizon of meaning, their cultural baggage, and the possibility of expressions of interpretation. The creative and imaginative potential of the educator at developing appreciation for literature in students can contribute significantly to instances of oral book clubs as a rewarding and imaginative body in the collective construction of aesthetic pleasure.

The importance of storytelling in cultures around the world dates back as far as humanity itself. The adoption of language marked a great cultural and historic turning point prompting the society about the relevance of language and its uses, the different sides of language. For long it was believed that writing and reading had the means to fix whatever was said, but it was with the advent of restructuring linguistics that society saw themselves submitting to transformation, placing writing and reading as indispensable abilities in the regimen of life itself. Likewise, literature and literacy must bear the mark of the semantic-relational function, making sense with the historical-social needs, contemplating the family, the school, and institutions. Teaching language is not therefore exclusively a school duty, that which is visible when we recognize the multiple stratifications that fill the students with problems well before they arrive. Therefore, it is condominium duty, radio, church, group, squares, in marches and demonstrations, since all that are guided by responsible adults, who care about the choice of words that will point to the ways of a literate and critical population.

## 7.2. Constructive Criticism

To provide constructive criticism, remember the rule of "feedback sandwich." In between layers of accolades and identifying strengths, have suggestions for improving weak areas. Any criticism should be thoughtful, specific, and gentle, and not simply fall to the other extreme of slash and burn. If you feel the need to open your letter with a disclaimer, explaining that the following might seem hurtful but that it's designed with positive intentions, that's your signal right there. If you're the one receiving constructive criticism, remember to stay open-minded and keep a thick skin. Understand that really, it's all your fault, but also note serious, helpful advice when you hear it.

7.2. Constructive criticism: The mantra is often "whatever makes you feel good," but constructive criticism is also vital to learning and growing as a writer. This involves not just patting somebody on the back and saying, "Good boy or girl," but helping them to develop and grow as a writer, even if that involves occasionally feeling bad. Constructive criticism is about helping a writer identify his or her weaknesses and work to overcome them, in addition to identifying his or her strengths so that he or she can build upon them. You don't learn to write effectively if you only hear that you're doing everything right. Having a weakness pointed out can be uncomfortable, and some of the most insecure writers might find it very hard to handle, but with the right feedback, it is essential to growth.

# CHAPTER 8

# Editing and Revising

The English word "edit" comes from the Latin edere, and was commonly used to refer to a review of a work in the publishing process. Editing involves carefully reading your paper and identifying a problem with grammar, usage, shape, form and style. Most problems are easy to identify and to correct, and they make your writing sound poor. Revising is an entirely different work as it involves re-seeing your work with a new vision and purpose. Editing is about formalities, of getting the craft and skill of writing, between what is said and the best way to it, sharing this knowledge and ability with the writer for the writer to make the final decision always keeping in mind her objective and her target readers. Always beginning with the fundamental principle of revision, who am I writing? But, the most important of all remember: the writer is the boss. Revision should be about possibilities, about seeing in various angles, about reading the text and re-writing the original, sharing new advancements in her text.

Editing involves proofreading your work to correct grammatical errors, to find and correct spelling mistakes. Revising your work helps develop and expand your ideas, allows you to see your writing from a different perspective, and so helps to interest and engage readers. Revisions and editing should come after you have written your first draft. This is also expecting and accepting critical feedback from your friends, family, and teachers. They must be honest but remember you can still choose to accept or reject their suggestions. When you trust one another, writing works because members are honest and receptive, not because the suggestions lead the writer to per se.

## 8.1. Proofreading

• Freshen up the verbiage with an eye for economy in your choice of words. For example: Do you really need to write "Do not be reluctant to complete your assignment in a timely manner", or is "Please complete your work on time" more to the point?

• Check that every word is perfect, with no typos. (Use Tools +W/ C). For example, if I mistakenly type "be hasty in sending off your work without proofreading", it can be accidentally spelled 'be nasty in...' Run the spellchecker after looking for hidden typos.

- Until spell-check is perfect, common sense rules: if you're writing about feisty fairies, the spell- and grammar-check will not recognize these names and so will mark them incorrect. You must be vigilant to identify false flags.

- Spell and grammar check is not infallible! If your spelling, etc., has issues, it will generate false reports. And spell-check will not pick up the error "The future looks impressive / The fuchsia looks impressive", or "faith" instead of "fate;" or many other problems. You must invest time and effort into this, to make sure every single word is perfect.

• Today's word-processing software comes complete with excellent spell and grammar check facilities. This makes those programs about three times more useful. Simply click the appropriate buttons and let the checker do its job.

• Check that all grammar and punctuation is perfect. (Practice this if you need to, as it is important if you wish to have your writing taken seriously).

8.1. Proofreading. Do not send in any assignment without proofreading it carefully first!

### 8.2. Refining Language

And that must find its space in your text. It's good to try to escape from that somewhat and use vehicle means to improve, to go beyond... I'm not saying that either choice of words is bad, but it's good to let the soul, the soul of the world that you're writing about, be expressed in an authentic way. Don't follow a recipe. It's good to have the idea of reading a lot and knowing very specific grammar rules, because that gives you a greater understanding of the language, but it's also very important to have your voice. Because we want to have the conclusion that when I read a text by such author, I know it's such author's text, even if it's something different, a unique theme. It's the narrative imprint. This is also very important. Often times people value spontaneity a lot but I think spontaneity in art is really chiselled, it's worked."

"Refining language: I think another thing that's very important about writing is the words we use to express ourselves. Once you have this idea of this image, there can be many different ways of expressing yourself. And for me, once I've written close to the text, for me the writing ends up with a precision that sometimes I don't know very well how to communicate. I mean, I'm trying to say that it's vital that you choose your words. It's very important that you show yourself, that you try to find... Things are so difficult to express... and it's very legitimate, very valid... One thing I always say when I'm being interviewed, when I'm at someone else's workshop, is that I'm very interested in authenticity, in what we are... deep down inside, the true personality of somebody.

# CHAPTER 9

# Publishing Your Work

In the nineties queer poets wanted to be published in publications that were as well, and a range of small magazines sprang up that nurtured the work of queer poets. I had the pleasure of working with other queer poets within those pages, and others didn't make such a connection. It wasn't a plan to exclude straight people per se, but to stretch the fabric of the conversation to the edge. If a straight person submitted a poem with political worth, worth that needed to be shared, and sought a little insertion on the edge of that conversation, or would help that existing dialogue be shared, then such poems would have been welcome. So when you have a poem in your possession that you wrote and need to send out, ask yourself not what magazine would be good for my poem, but what poem will be good for the magazine. Then you have to be smart about your submission; one bullet will hit the target, not a scatter gun attack. Research the sites, take their temperature, do a pre-flight check, and a routine. Know the editors, know the nature of the poets whose work also features. Also know that your work has value and has something to offer.

You have a selection of your work, tidied it up, polished it, and we know that we can send stuff off to places; and now we are going to think about the places you can try sending it to. I have talked to some poets who write amazing poems, but the few they send out only go to five or six magazines. These guys are letting the side down. If creative writing is a conversation, you have got to listen in and answer on the same wavelength that already exists. Therefore, finding the magazines and presses that have the conversation most suitable to the poem you have written is essential.

### 9.1. Self-Publishing

In the "Good Old Days" prior to 2005, many writers used to mail typewritten or printed manuscripts to publishers who would return the works if they were lucky in a few months with a polite "No thanks". A few weeks later, after continued rejections by other potential publishers, the discouraging ritual was repeated. Authors would make enough copies in one submission to mail to all interested publishers or wait many weeks for the photocopiers at their full-time job or the drop in copy shop prices on the day when money and time permitted for the major output printing day. Now, fortunately, writers can email their 12 pt. typed papers in specific electronic formats to many publishers as an illustration of their work, query them in advance, or submit book proposals to motivated publishers.

Self-publishing; Becoming an Author and Connecting with Your Audience: Many authors find that they get their biggest thrill from seeing their book in print and/or available for their targeted audience. Today, relatively inexpensive digital desktop printing and online publishers allow greater opportunities for authors to bypass the traditional New York publishing houses, which often want more control and a bigger piece of the financial pie. At the least, authors may want to consider alternative publishers or print-on-demand options to retain more control and obtain greater percentages of every book sale. Writers can publish and sell their works on the internet, rent small presses for small print runs, peddle their books at speaking engagements, pre-sell their works, crowdfund a project, set up affiliations with related groups or businesses, announce and find support on Facebook, and prepare for vending opportunities at related fairs, workshops, and conferences.

*9.2. Traditional Publishing*

Creative Writing Workshop: Ignite Your Imagination. Writing is therapeutic and can lead to greater self-awareness. It's also a rewarding experience, but it can be frustrating at times. Sometimes your best writing days come few and far between. In this article Jetse de Vries introduces ten secrets for writing that relationship-building story. Writing is a deep and powerful form of communication. It is a bond that brings people together and allows us to surround ourselves with others who care for and understand us. Writers are artists who urge their readers to take a closer look at society and at themselves. They express their unique vision and alter our perception of what is real and what is possible. Writers encourage others to think, to feel, to live. Writers shape the world. All of us have the potential to write. We can all blow life into the pages we create. We all have our own realities, observations and observations. We all have something to say. It takes time, method and effort to express our feelings and our views about the world accurately, to find the right words and deliver our message.

Traditional publishing. E-publishing is a wonderful thing, but don't get so gung-ho about it that you overlook a traditional publisher. So how do you go about getting your book published by a traditional publisher? 1. Write a book that's worth publishing. Contrary to popular belief, publishers are not desperate to publish any old rubbish; they want to publish a good book. So find yourself a creative writing course, spend a few months (or even years) honing your craft and then start writing.

# CHAPTER 10

# Conclusion

I can appreciate all the students who attended this workshop because they have a huge potential for creativity. I believe that for the student to be fully creative, the esteem of teachers and others does not need to be appealing. Teachers must favor opportunities to create, apply all the techniques of joint creation, creativity feedback, perseverance and discipline; make it safe; inspire curiosity, open their minds to new ideas, and help students really believe in themselves. Finally, thank you very much to all the creative writers who participated in this workshop, and I hope that all the values generated in the creative writing experiences can create expertise in your professional and social life. I end this workshop with the certainty that we can learn a lot from students and creative writers' writing if we review language issues and apply creative exercises that consider children's oral and written cultural values. Put these creative exercises in practice and see how exciting it is to teach creative grammar.

Congratulations! You have completed this Creative Writing Workshop: Ignite Your Imagination. I hope that through this workshop you have learned key concepts and educational ideas from writing, to contribute to three professional groups: teachers, students, and creative writers. As educators, we occupy a privileged place in creative dispositions in our students and in our social groups. In the classroom, by creating rich interaction environments, we can teach with joy, a main driver of creativity. Besides the sensations of pleasure and satisfaction, the feeling that we can take new knowledge, new ideas, classes that find a solution to both new situations and problems is the feeling of creativity. In the creative process, it means when creative thoughts are put into action, produce tangible ideas and objects of indirect evaluation, understanding and value for a society. As this workshop comes to an end, keep in mind that all these writing experiences with creativity can be included in at least two domains of education: linguistic communication and arts. Thereupon, encourage your own creativity in pedagogical practice. caregiving scenarios that make students safe and capable creators.

## 10.1. Final Thoughts

Allow me to leave you with this thought—ignite your imagination and you are guiding the process of creation. The world (and all the available human senses) is your inspiration. Every day we come face to face with water lilies and fire trucks, curtains and highways, plastic bags and old bicycles. Many of us are drawn to record and preserve our vision of such day-to-day things. Likewise, much of what eventually surfaces in the arts is in fact inspired by what resides in the world. Your imagination becomes so much the more powerful when the world has become your source of inspiration. True inspiration and creativity comes when you observe, interact with, and interpret the world around you.

When you pick up a pen, you have just as much chance of being the successful writer as anyone else. The only idea you now have to deal with is this: Your writing abilities haven't been burnt out of you, your creative imagination remains as vibrant and strong as it was when you were a child. How do we keep this date alive, on this, the very last day of our course? The answer, my friends, is imagination.

It is amazing and awe-inspiring that each of us has the capacity to write. Each of us is capable of putting pen to paper and seeing our thoughts solidify into something more; expressed, the nebulous becomes the possible. The amazing and incredible thing about this potential is this—it never goes away. Our capability to write? It stays with us our whole lives. No matter what your job is, no matter your occupation, your address or your place in life – none of that matters. We are all endowed with the capacity to think, perceive, formulate thoughts, and express those thoughts through the written word.

www.ingramcontent.com/pod-product-compliance
Lightning Source LLC
Chambersburg PA
CBHW021406160726
47994CB00007B/3096